# A Birthday Pa

by Laurel Dickey

Pioneer Valley Educational Press, Inc.

Mom got candy.

Mom got a present.

Mom got hats.

Mom got balloons.

Mom got plates.

Mom got a card.

Mom got pizza.

Mom got forks.

Mom got cups.

Mom got napkins.

Mom got ice cream.

Mom got spoons.

Mom got a cake.

# Happy birthday to you!